THE Bl   O

SKIING

David Allsop

Colette House
52-55 Piccadilly
London W1J 0DX
United Kingdom

Email: info@bluffers.com
Website: bluffers.com
Twitter: @BluffersGuide

First published 1992
This edition published 2012
Copyright © Bluffer's® 2012

Publisher: Thomas Drewry
Publishing Director: Brooke McDonald

Series Editor: David Allsop
Design and Illustration by Jim Shannon

A CIP Catalogue record for this book
is available from the British Library.

Bluffer's Guide®, Bluffer's® and Bluff Your Way®
are registered trademarks.

ISBN: 978-1-909365-00-1 (print)
      978-1-909365-01-8 (ePub)
      978-1-909365-02-5 (Kindle)

CONTENTS

All skiers, irrespective of their age,
sex or ability, like to pretend that they
are better skiers than they actually are.

THE SLIPPERY SLOPE

Skiing requires a commitment to pleasure of the sort endorsed by hedonists, layabouts, ne'er-do-wells and philanderers – in other words, a single-minded approach to absolute self-indulgence.

Skiers are deeply flawed people, so it will come as no surprise that most of them are also extremely proficient bluffers. All skiers will remember that triumphant moment when they first skied down to a crowded restaurant terrace without falling over. Flushed with pride, they will have puffed up their chests in the fond belief that onlookers were bursting with admiration. In fact, onlookers were doing nothing of the sort, waiting patiently instead for someone else to fall over so that they could point at them and jeer.

But in that brief moment of triumph, the discerning novice will have discovered a profound truth about skiing. All skiers, irrespective of their age, sex or ability, like to pretend that they are better skiers than they actually are. That axiom lies at the root of the sport, and from that root flourishes the most luxuriant verbiage of preposterous declarations about imagined skills and expertise.

This book will offer a few hints and techniques that will allow you to be accepted as a skier of rare ability and experience. But it will do more. It will give you the tools to impress legions of marvelling listeners with your knowledge and advice – without anyone discovering that you can't ski to save your life.

HOW IT ALL STARTED

The British always claim to have invented alpine skiing, a remarkable feat bearing in mind the paucity of Alps in the British Isles. But let's not split hairs. Alpine skiing, the most popular variety of the three main forms of the sport, is that particular discipline that involves skiing downhill. Skiing along on a level gradient is known by those who find it tedious as 'poling' or by those who find it interesting as 'cross-country' or 'Nordic' skiing (possibly invented and, unaccountably, enjoyed hugely by Norwegians).

Uphill skiing is widely described either as 'ski touring' or, by those rash enough to attempt it, as 'absolutely bloody exhausting'.

The British did, in fact, invent alpine skiing – but were not the first to spot the potential of binding wooden planks to their feet as a means of transport. That responsibility lies with the Swedes, or possibly the Finns, or possibly the Laps, or the Norwegians, maybe even the Russians. The Mongols and Turks are also keen to state their own case for having invented it. So too are the Chinese. Sinologists will happily produce ancient manuscripts that mention *mu-ma* – literally, men on 'wooden horses' travelling at the speed of a galloping thoroughbred across the Manchurian plains. This suggests that even during the Tang dynasty (618-906 AD), primitive skiers on primitive equipment could happily have seen off the British Olympic downhill team.

The oldest 'ski' in existence was found in a peat bog in Hoting, Sweden, and dates from 2500 BC. Some cave drawings dating from about the same time showing hunters on skis have been found in Rødøy, Norway. But it wasn't until the 1820s that skiing came into its own as a sport when the Norwegians began cavorting about in the snow on skis. They loved it. By the middle of the century they were holding cross-country races for 'gentlemen'. Then, in a competition in Oslo in 1868, a farmhand called Sondre Norheim turned up and spoiled everyone's fun by winning every race. The secret of his success was a ski he had designed himself, with a 'waist' and a secure binding.

Sondre sank without trace but his invention found its way to the Great Exhibition in Paris in 1889. One interested purchaser was a doctor from Switzerland who took the new skis back to Davos, put them in his attic then forgot about them. A few years later they were discovered by his apprentice, Tobias Branger, and he and his brother became known as the Davos 'plank-hoppers'.

Nobody took them too seriously until Sir Arthur Conan Doyle turned up one day in 1894 and asked to be shown how to plank-hop. The Branger brothers took him over the mountain pass to Arosa and Sir Arthur was smitten. Writing in *Strand Magazine* a short while later he observed prophetically: 'I am convinced that the time will come when hundreds of Englishmen will come to Switzerland for the "skiing" season.'

Sure enough, Sir Henry Lunn, inventor of the modern package holiday, arrived in the early 1900s with his newly founded Public Schools Alpine Sports Club and promptly colonised the Swiss Alps with carefully selected members of the British upper classes. The bemused Swiss claimed that they needed a passport to get into their own towns and villages.

Within a few years there was barely
a skiable mountain in the Alps
that didn't have a train going up it,
round it or through it.

The British then insisted their diligent hosts find ways to get them to the top of mountains with the minimum of fuss. They demanded that trains be installed, or else. This is where the Swiss came into their own because, as everyone knows, they like trains a lot. Within a few years there was barely a skiable mountain in the Alps that didn't have a train going up it, round it or through it. Once at the top, the British would get out, put on their skis and hare off to the bottom, making as much noise as possible. Previously, the whole point of skiing had been to get from one point to another – and nobody could see the point of going halfway, then coming back, then doing it all over again.

Nevertheless it caught on, albeit as an elitist pastime, practised exclusively by people with nasal voices and no chins. The splendidly egalitarian Swiss soon put a stop to that when Zurich engineer Ernst Constam arrived in Davos in 1934 and invented the cheap-to-install drag lift (*see* T-bars, page 39) – the only form of uphill transport designed with the explicit purpose of jettisoning its passengers without warning. Suddenly the slopes were invaded by the world's great unwashed – keen to spend vast amounts of money (something else the Swiss like a lot). The British retired to their mountain hotels grumbling that, yet again, someone had stolen their idea and ruined it.

SKIING CLUBS

There are only two skiing clubs that you really need to know about: the Kandahar and the DHO. The Kandahar Ski Club was founded in 1924 by Sir Arnold Lunn, Henry's son, in Mürren, Switzerland. It was named after Field Marshal Lord Roberts of Kandahar, Afghanistan, who apparently knew a thing or two about mountains. Some idea of the spirit of the club comes from an account of one of its early meetings. Casting around for a suitable badge or emblem, founder member AH d'Egville suggested a simple 'K'. 'But nobody will know what the "K" means,' reasoned a fellow member.

'If they want to find out what "K" means', thundered Eggy, 'they can bloody well find out for themselves.'

The DHO (Downhill Only) Club was founded a year later directly across the valley in neighbouring Wengen. Here, the admission policy was a little more relaxed and the occasional native of Wengen was allowed to join. The then mayor of Wengen, one Dr Zahnd, observed proudly of his fellow citizens that they had 'learned from the British, not only to race and to battle but also to lose'. They must have been profoundly grateful for this lesson.

There has been no love lost between the DHO and the Kandahar. Like any other club, the sole purpose of both is to form a gang and tell other people that they can't join.

The only other ski club of any relevance is the Ski Club of Great Britain. Founded in London by some early downhillers, it started by being very posh, but these days almost anyone can join, which rather defeats the object. You must also be able to talk about two other clubs. The first ever to be formed was the Kiandra Snow Shoe Club in the Snowy Mountains of Australia in 1861, founded by Norwegians. It quickly went the same way as the Tasmanian Tiger (out of existence), so make up as much as you want to about it.

The other notable club was the curiously named Yukki, founded by some young British officers at the St Petersburg embassy in Russia in the late 1800s. Its main aim was to hunt bearskins for the regiment's hats, but from all accounts the bears remained relatively untroubled by their dashing predators.

HOW SKIING SPREAD

It is generally accepted that mass labour migrations from Scandinavia during the nineteenth century account for the spread of skiing in the USA, Australia and New Zealand. This does not, however, account for how it made its way to Morocco, India, Japan and Chile – but let's not be picky.

Skiing had a more practical purpose in the USA. In California a skiing postman delivered the mail over the Sierras in the 1850s. And in Telluride, Colorado, on payday at the Tomboy mine 3,000 feet above town, the Finns and Swedes would strap on makeshift skis with grim determination and infuriate their co-workers by getting down to the dozen brothels before them.

SKI TERRAIN

SLOPES AND GRADING

Slopes are called slopes or 'runs' or 'pistes' in Europe, 'trails' in the USA, and whatever anybody feels like calling them in Australia and New Zealand. Beginners will be relieved to discover that there are different gradients of slopes. They range from 'easy' to 'absurdly dangerous' and are graded by colour according to degree of difficulty. Thus a 'green' slope is perceived to be easy, a 'blue' is less easy, a 'red' less easy still, and a 'black' is no place for bluffers.

All runs have 'piste-markers' – appropriately coloured signs ingeniously placed to cause maximum obstruction. Black runs often have additional signs bearing the legend 'For experts only'. These prove irresistible to those who fondly imagine themselves to be experts but aren't. On no account fall victim to the same temptation. There may be opportunities when nobody is looking to paint a blue sign black and transplant the 'experts only' sign to a blue run. Later, you can plunge past shouting 'Geronimo!' to your startled friends.

In the USA and Canada they don't have red runs. It might have something to do with an unhappy association with the colour of blood. Their absence is compensated for by black runs that in Europe would be graded as red. To complete the North American picture there are two types of black run – 'single' and 'double diamonds'. Double diamonds are the ones to avoid. Some resorts also have two types of green and blue piste as well as off-piste.

The terms 'on-piste' and 'off-piste' have delighted headline writers for years. 'Piste-off' is a favourite for journalists trying to be witty about some calamity that has taken place on their 'familiarisation visits' (free ski trips). This usually has something to do with having to buy their own drinks.

Moguls are big bumps in the snow.
In the USA they are called,
with admirable inventiveness, bumps.

In fact, skiing 'on-piste' involves staying on marked runs that have been prepared ('groomed' in the USA) and made safe by 'piste-bashers' or 'snowcats' – machines resembling a cross between a tank and a combine harvester that emit a bleeping noise to warn of their presence (a noise invariably turned off when they approach blind bends).

Piste-bashers, and other assorted snow-grooming

machinery, earned a certain notoriety in *On Her Majesty's Secret Service* when James Bond ski-jumped over one and the baddy following him didn't.* There followed a great deal of grinding and squirting of blood and gristle which had cinema audiences around the world stamping their feet and applauding. Ever since, drivers of these sinister machines have behaved as if they have a licence to mince.

After piste-bashers have done their worst, the surface is like corrugated iron and about as easy to ski on. That's why many people prefer to ski off-piste ('off-limits' in the USA) – that part of the mountain that is ungroomed, unmarked, frequently prone to avalanches and, if it's a glacier, crevasses. An increasing number of skiers prefer to take their chances with these natural hazards rather than take on four tons of metal and a Magimix.

Serious skiers never admit to skiing on-piste, unless as a means of getting off-piste. If you are on your way to ski off-piste, make great show of the fact by shouting loudly to nobody in particular: 'Franz! Have you got a spare pair of powder straps?'

MOGULS

Moguls are big bumps in the snow. In the USA they are called, with admirable inventiveness, bumps. They are caused by successive skiers turning in the same spot, pushing the snow into hard, compact piles. If you hit one of these piles at speed, you will soar about 20 feet into the

* For more 007-related bluffing, see *The Bluffer's Guide to Bond*.

air before landing on your back with your ski in your ear. It is difficult to pretend that you did this on purpose.

There is a certain type of skier who claims to 'love' moguls. Nobody loves moguls, unless they are bluffing, in which case they must be accorded proper respect. This means that you must love them, too. When you fall over, claim that an old ligament rupture (*see* Injuries, page 55) prevented you from 'achieving full absorption'.

PATHS

Paths are generally strewn liberally with rocks and black ice. On one side they have jagged cliff walls which invite your close attention; on the other side they have vertiginous drops through more rocks and splintered conifers. The splintering was caused by skiers.

Take careful note of where paths are and try to plan a route that avoids them. This is most important, because everyone's natural inclination on a path is to adopt the snowplough position, drag their poles between their legs and whimper loudly. Bluffers cannot afford to be seen doing this.

Instructors will tell you that it's all about psychology and that the secret with paths is to pretend that they're not there. Ignore this advice. Instructors don't get caught in the conifers.

PISTE MAPS

Nobody has yet invented a piste map that returns to its original folds. In the USA they are called 'trail maps' and have up to 148 folds. These are the most advanced types and were allegedly invented by Rubik. Not even he can solve their limitless capacity to outwit.

Piste maps are supposed to show skiers where to go in clear, comprehensive, cartographical detail. Thus they bear little relation to a mountainside. In unfamiliar territory it is wise to allow someone else to take the initiative, then scoff mercilessly when you get lost.

VERTICAL DROPS

An arresting feature of mountainous terrain, the term 'vertical drop' actually describes two different things:

1. what will happen if you fail to stop at the edge of a sheer cliff face; or

2. the distance in height between the top ski 'station' and the bottom (usually the resort).

For some reason the latter usage greatly challenges putative experts. Venture knowledgeably therefore that the biggest 'vertical' in the Alps is down the Vallée Blanche from the Aiguille du Midi to Chamonix (about 2,750 metres or nearly two vertical miles); and, in the Rockies, Blackcomb to Whistler (about 1,600 metres), known as The Vertical Mile.

Don't expect to survive a vertical drop of the first sort much over 10 metres.

Zips, buckles, epaulettes, superfluous pockets, pockets on pockets, braid, fur and loud insignia combine to deliver a compelling and unmistakable message: 'This person cannot ski.'

CLOTHES AND EQUIPMENT

What you wear when you are skiing or, more importantly, when you are not skiing but hanging around trying to look as if you are about to start skiing, is an intrinsic part of successful bluffing.

Zips, buckles, epaulettes, superfluous pockets, pockets on pockets, braid, fur and loud insignia combine to deliver a compelling and unmistakable message. They have the same effect as a neon sign flashing the words: 'This person cannot ski.' The wise are not seduced by fashion mores and know the value of eschewing glitz and wearing old, suitably battered ski-clothes. Onlookers will leap immediately to the conclusion that you have been skiing for years. A useful role model for bluffers is the character played by Kirk Douglas in *The Heroes of Telemark*, who sported a terrific blue anorak and a leather belt with grenades hanging off it. The grenades are not de rigueur unless you find yourself skiing in the Hindu Kush.

Those fortunate enough to have ancient skiing relatives could profit from searching attics and old trunks. Nothing cuts a finer dash on the slopes than the original 'Golden

Age of Skiing' look, popular in the 1920s – best exemplified by Oliver Reed's character in the film *Women in Love*.

If all else fails, there is a ready-made and little-known market for authentic-looking, second-hand skiwear and – this is the clever part – you get to look like even more of an expert when you wear it. Many local instructors and guides are required to change their ski apparel every season and therefore have trunkloads of the stuff lying around at home. Utterly baffled as to why anybody should be interested in their old ski clothes, they are easily persuaded to part with their soiled Gore-Tex for bargain prices. Often they omit to take off their official badges, which means that you can masquerade as an expert as long as you don't go anywhere near their resort again. Or any slope anywhere.

A bewildering amount of nonsense is talked about skis, bindings and poles. This is therefore fertile territory for bluffers, but it is an area where a comprehensive knowledge of ski-talk is desirable.

SKIS

Skis used to be made out of wood but are now made from an apparently infinite variety of materials with zappy names. All new skis boast the most remarkable technological advances ever achieved in the history of modern science. This must be true because upwards of 2,000 new models come on to the market every season and they all claim to render last year's skis obsolete – a sound enough argument for never buying new skis but renting and ruining somebody else's instead.

Beware ski salespeople who know their stuff or sound as if they do. A typical conversation in a ski shop will go something like this:

Prospective purchaser (modestly) Can you please recommend a good 'all-round' ski for someone of average ability?

Salesperson Lucky you came in this afternoon, Sir/Madam. We've just laid our hands on the only pair of the Bionic-Zelcron Turbo Explosion Ultima left in the world. It's unquestionably the best ski ever made.

Prospective purchaser I see. Why?

Salesperson (taking a deep breath) Unlike any other ski ever made, this latest Ultima has a Zelcron multi-layer vacuum sandwich construction ensuring maximum torsional rigidity yet balanced longitudinal flex, coupled with a ketone-Kevlar microcell core, Z900 graphite base, V12 tapered torsion box, asymmetric gate deflector, trapezoid sidewalls, directional dampers and an ultra-slim slalom sidecut which, all in all, will guarantee that Sir/Madam instantly becomes the best skier in the world. These babies will cut through concrete.

Prospective purchaser Hmm. Have you got them in pink?

Salesperson Of course. Sir/Madam shows excellent taste. That will be £650, please.

Ski salespeople are fluent in 'ski-tech' in at least 10 languages. Take careful note of what they say and repeat it *ad nauseam* when defending your particular choice. In most cases, the choice is determined by aesthetic considerations. Modern skis bear the most extraordinarily vulgar graphics. In a rare exception to the 'non-neon' rule, be as vulgar as you can afford to be in this department – as long as they don't have 'turbo' written on them anywhere.

There are only three things that you really need to know about downhill skis:

1. There should be two of them (unless you happen to be one-legged).

2. They should match (not essential, but desirable).

3. They should move forward when you stand on them pointing downhill.

But there are other important little titbits that can be dropped carefully into the conversation to show your mastery of the subject. Foremost among these is the uncontestable fact that skis are either 'hard', 'soft' or somewhere in between. A hard ski is difficult to bend; a soft ski is not.

The enquiring skier will demand to know why there should be a difference. This has something to do with how a ski distributes its load along its 'camber' and how this affects its ability to turn. Simply remember that a hard ski distributes the weight of the skier evenly along its length, thus making it better for skiing on hard snow.

In soft snow it is desirable for the tip to 'float', so a soft ski that concentrates the load in the ski's mid-section is apparently better for turning. There is a useful mnemonic to aid memory: 'Soft snow, soft ski. Hard snow, hard ski.' It is the basis of all ski technology.

There is a time-honoured way of testing ski stiffness that may impress bystanders. Hold the ski upright, put one foot against the bottom and, holding it by the middle with one hand, pull the top towards you with the other. This will show how flexible it is, in the unlikely event that anybody is interested in knowing. If it snaps in half it clearly wasn't worth having in the first place.

♛

Claiming to have 'blunt edges' is a
valid excuse for most forms
of skiing ineptitude.

'Edges' – the sharp metal bits on the side of the ski that grip the snow – are also something with which you should be familiar. If they are not sharp, they will not work. If they don't work, you will fall over. It is important that they be sharpened for effective 'edging' so you can 'carve' proper turns (*see* Technique) and stay upright as much as possible. A useful knack for gauging the right degree of sharpness is to run a fingernail across them. If a bit of nail is shaved off, things are fine. If not, you have a valid excuse for sliding uncontrollably about the mountainside. Claiming to have 'blunt edges' is a valid excuse for most forms of skiing ineptitude.

Another way to blame your skis for your semi-permanent prostration is to claim that their 'soles' or 'bases' are gouged, or rough, or not properly waxed. Surprisingly, there may be some element of justification in this claim. Worn running surfaces will adversely affect performance, so take no chances and get your skis fully 'tuned' as soon as you can – but never admit to having had a 'tuning', in case it makes absolutely no difference to your skiing. And don't worry too much about 'waxing'. Having the base waxed (*le fart* in French) tends to alarm many skiers who imagine that a more 'slippery' ski will be more difficult to control. In fact, the reverse is true – so you can wax away to your heart's content and convince yourself that your skiing is improving as a result.

The right length of ski is also a critical area. It is tempting to assume that length is somehow proportional to ability, and a common mistake is to buy or rent the longest ski in the shop. This is probably because the longer the ski is, the faster it goes. But however strong the temptation to demand a '210' (the longest non-competition size), resist it if you're planning to survive until après-ski. Skis over 200cm should only be used by heavy experts or people who aren't planning to turn, or stop, at any stage of their descent (generally known as 'racers', 'speed-skiers' or 'nutters'). If asked what length of ski you prefer, simply ensure that they measure somewhere between your chin and the top of your head.

Those who have always felt that a shorter ski would

be more suited to their level of incompetence have been rewarded by the introduction of 'carving' skis. Carvers, which now account for nearly 100% of all ski production, are much wider at the tip and tail than their predecessors (see 'sidecut' in Glossary), up to 50cm shorter than traditional skis and thus a lot easier to manoeuvre. About time, too. Designed to take the effort out of 'carving' a turn, they are a godsend to skiers who have never quite come to terms with the concept of making any sort of turn in the first place. Note that some purists insist on sticking with old-style models. However tempting this is for bluffers, don't fall victim to it. They are virtually impossible to ski on once you have tried carving skis. Well, you can ski, but you can't turn.

Finally, the way skis are carried says much about their carrier. There is only one proper way to carry skis, and that is base to base, over one shoulder, with the tips pointing towards the ground. This looks better than any other way. There is no other reason for it.

BINDINGS

Bindings are the devices that hold the boots on to the skis. As long as they are in reasonable condition there is little to choose between them in terms of how they affect performance. The most important function they have is to 'release' the ski when the skier is cartwheeling gracefully down the slope. If they do not release the ski, you will be unable to put any weight on your leg(s) for about three months.

Like skis, bindings have their own arcane vernacular. Thus, if you are planning to buy some, you will hear a great deal about equalisers, inclined pivots, upper-boot radius, lateral elasticity, power relays, anti-friction devices and cam triggers.

Feel free to bandy these terms about; most skiers haven't an inkling what they mean either. The only bits of the binding you should be able to recognise are the 'toe units', 'heel units' and 'brakes'. The only term you actually need be familiar with is 'binding'.

The toe unit holds or releases the front of the boot, the heel unit does the same to the rear and the brakes stop the ski skidding down the mountain when it falls off. The brakes have nothing to do with slowing the rate of descent; that is only achieved by proper 'edging'. Or by colliding with a stationary object.

You are advised not to get too carried away with your expertise on bindings and certainly not to the extent of tampering with the binding 'settings' yourself. This should be adjusted by someone who knows what he or she is doing. There is no need to admit to knowing nothing about how to adjust them. Simply say, if asked, that you haven't got the right 'tool' and that for 'safety reasons' you prefer not to ski with bindings that haven't been tested on a torque gauge – sinister-looking machines with clamps, mechanical twists and computer printouts. They were probably invented by Torquemada.

Try to adopt one habit before slotting into your bindings. Always tap the sole of the boot hard with your ski pole to dislodge compacted snow or mud, or scrape the sole against the binding in a pendulum motion. Experts do this to guard against 'pre-release' (*see* Glossary), so you should too.

POLES

Poles are what skiers call the long, spindly sticks that they carry with them and sometimes remember to 'plant' in the snow. Never call them sticks, nor leave them in the snow on the rare occasions you remember to plant them.

Like skis, poles are usually made of some fabulously advanced scientific material. They consist of three component parts: the 'shaft', the 'grip' or handle, and the 'basket'. The basket is the most interesting part because it not only has a useful function – preventing the pole from burying itself up to the hilt in the snow – but also because its name is frequently forgotten.

Handles come in a variety of 'sculpted', 'notched' or 'protective' shapes. The shape isn't remotely important. However, try to get hold of a pole with a 'shock absorber' between its handle and shaft and insist that they 'really do make a difference on compression turns'.

Shafts should be bent as soon as possible. This not only shows that you have been 'planting' them often and hard but that you have experienced a few spectacular crashes. Bending a pole can either be achieved by using your knee as a brace, by buying them ready-bent (called 'corrective angles') or by falling on them.

BOOTS

Notwithstanding that after a day's skiing they smell worse than an old mackerel, ski boots are vital pieces of equipment. It has to be conceded, however, that they offer all the buckles, knobs, flashes, clips and levers that the discerning foot-fetishist requires – none of which will single out the wearer as a person of questionable taste or habits.

Ski boots used to fall into three categories: the alarming-sounding 'rear-entry', the more innocuous-sounding 'mid-entry' and the traditional 'front-entry'. These days they all share a common entry, which is the top bit under the tongue – in other words, a top entry. Like skis, ski boots are now either stiff or soft. The latter are easily distinguished by the mesh-like material spanning the forefoot and 'throat' of the boot (a useful word when trying to impress boot fitters). This is supposed to make the boot more comfortable but, as all boots have the comfort characteristics of a heavy-duty industrial clamp, it is unlikely to be the case.

The notion of comfort is sneered at by experts, who expect to suffer for their sport, and therefore it must be sneered at by bluffers. Claim confidently that it significantly compromises the vital requirements of close 'feel' for the terrain, power thrust (whatever that means) and efficient energy transmission between shell and ski. There is a useful verb to bandy about, as in: 'I prefer a stiffer performance boot which "holds" like a cat on a living room curtain.' If asked what exactly it 'holds' on to, answer contemptuously: 'The snow, stupid.'

But beware a boot of any sort with too many clips and fiddly bits, however tempting it might be to claim that these alluring gizmos are essential for 'fine-tuning'. A degree in engineering is required to understand them – or even to get into the boot in the first place – and you run the risk of exhibiting all the classic symptoms of obsessive-compulsive behaviour by tweaking and adjusting the settings constantly.

Boots are useful things to blame if your skiing technique is exposed to unflattering critical scrutiny. Pointing accusingly at the offending items, you can say: 'I just can't get enough forward (or lateral) flex.' On the other hand, a boot of the wrong size can render you unable even to think about who or what to blame. Ski-boot pain enters a different dimension of suffering. Chafed calves, bloodless toes, suppurating blisters, mind-numbing cramps, bruises on bruises and toenails that curl up like poppadoms are traumas that every skier will endure at some time – and these are some of the more bearable privations. There is no such thing as a comfortable ski boot; just concentrate on finding one that doesn't make you pray for a merciful death.

Furthermore, the admission of ski-boot agony suggests the probability of inexperience. Experts never whinge about their boots. Bluffers just starting out should hire boots and have no compunction about taking them back to the shop at the first sign of distress. Try out every pair in the resort, and if you find one that doesn't drive you to suicide, sell everything you own to acquire it.

BAGS

For those committed enough to buy their own boots and skis, there are certain guidelines to follow when choosing luggage. If you are unable to find something pre-used, send newly purchased bags to yourself via the Royal Mail – a parcel service that has perfected the art of achieving an instant 'distressed' look.

Original canvas and leather bags, proudly exhibited by descendants of Golden Age skiers, are at an absolute premium and cannot be purchased for realistic prices. If, by dint of extraordinary good fortune, you come across some, buy or purloin them immediately. They will ensure admiring glances forever.

Battered rucksacks are equally desirable, especially if they look as if they have been scraped along some serious terrain. As with bags, there is an easy way of conveying this high-credibility impression. If you can't wait for the Royal Mail to get around to delivering them, fill them with rocks, tie them to the bumper of your car and tow them around for a day or two.

VITAL-TO-BE-AVOIDED CLOTHING

There are certain basic rules for bluffers to observe with clothing. Never wear any of the following: a hat with ears, or any sort of headband with your name on the front, especially if it's Helmut or Adolf; Lycra racing pants (especially if you have a large behind); or salopettes (dungaree-type trousers that prove impossible to remove when you are overtaken by necessity). In addition, take particular care never to wear white (not easy to see on the slopes), however much you may be tempted to pass yourself off as a member of der Alpenkorps. The advantages of professed membership of this august and glamorous body (which got soundly whacked by *The Heroes of Telemark*) are significantly outweighed by the tendency of everybody else on the mountain to ski into you at speed.

USEFUL BLUFFING IMPEDIMENTA

Extreme accoutrements (none of which you will ever actually need) will reinforce your credibility. They should be sported ostentatiously and occasionally fingered thoughtfully as you recount another of your highly creative anecdotes. Try any of the following:

The flashiest avalanche transceiver you can find This is a device that sends out a feeble signal to rescuers some time after you have been buried. In most cases it would be quicker to wait for the snow to melt.

An impact-triggered balloon Designed to 'float' you to the top of a loose-snow avalanche travelling faster than a Formula One racing car.

A telescopic-handled shovel Supposedly useful in an avalanche but equally useful if you can't find a mountain lavatory (*see* salopettes, previously).

An avalanche 'probe' A long, bendy thing for locating bodies under the snow; also useful for prodding people awake when your anecdotes render them comatose.

A sniffer dog Your best chance of being discovered if you actually do get buried in an avalanche. Their extraordinary ability to detect someone buried many feet beneath the snow (especially those with a pocketful of Cheesy Wotsits) has saved many an avalanche victim.

The downhill equivalent of a violent shank into the clubhouse is an uncontrolled sliding stop into a lift queue.

ADVANCED BLUFFING ACCOUTREMENTS

Like golf, a recreation that is equally inviting to those of us who are prone to fantasising about imagined expertise*, downhill snowsports have an unfortunate tendency to expose deficiencies in the cruellest way. The difference is that the downhill equivalent of a violent shank into the clubhouse (before a keenly judgmental audience of fellow so-called experts) is an uncontrolled sliding stop into a lift queue. There is no legitimate excuse for flattening fellow skiers in these circumstances, except one. Simply withdraw a large radio transmitter from some part of your clothing and shout into the mouthpiece: 'Did you get that? Or do we need to shoot it again?' Most people become surprisingly forgiving if they think they're on camera

* See *The Bluffer's Guide to Golf*.

and become positively eager to please if you happen to mention that you're a stunt double for Tom Cruise. If you really want to push your luck, point back up the mountain and say that he's following closely behind you with the rest of the film crew. Then move effortlessly to the front of the queue while their attention is otherwise occupied.

A two-way radio is therefore a useful part of the slope-cred armoury. It doesn't need to work, just as long as it makes a convincing crackling noise. It doesn't even have to be a radio, so long as it's big and black, suitably battered and preferably held together with elephant tape. It's always a good idea to insert into it a very small shortwave radio tuned into the North Korean World Service (somewhere around 479kHz). This is usually rendered completely indecipherable by helpful static, along with the added benefit that nobody will be able to understand any of the occasional words that make it through the ether. A fat, and completely unnecessary, wavy aerial is also handy because it suggests that you regularly venture into remote parts of the mountain on dangerously exciting expeditions. Seasoned mountain veterans like guides and pisteurs invariably sport such devices ostentatiously in holsters or breast pockets. You should therefore follow their example – better still, offer them hard cash for the entire package and chuck in your mobile (which has nil bluffing credibility on a mountain) to clinch the deal.

The radio will complement your other credibility-enhancing equipment such as a shovel, avalanche transceiver, probe and balloon pack (as previously recommended), and means that you can draw attention to yourself by shouting nonsense into it whenever you feel a need to impress someone. Useful phrases include things like: 'I'm going to blow the cornice on peak two' – in any language you choose. (Don't forget to say 'Over' when you finish.)

But there is one further item that will immeasurably raise your status on the slopes. A large, shoulder-mounted 35mm film camera is an invaluable investment for advanced bluffers. Not only does it attract admiring glances from aspiring starlets, it also provides you with a perfect excuse for skiing or boarding with all the speed and grace of a pack mule. Like the radio, it doesn't have to work, and will improve your image further if it looks as if it's been over a few cliffs. The film camera ploy has further advantages: many ski resorts will bend over backwards to accommodate a film crew. All you have to do is invest in some suitably authentic-looking business cards, equip your mates with long sticks with furry-hatted microphones on the end, maybe an arc light or two, a big disc covered in BacoFoil, a clapperboard of course, and – as if by magic – you will acquire instant credibility, not to mention free skiing for about six of you.

Finally, there is one skiing accessory that eclipses all others. It is known as the 'ski sleb'. It involves a bit of basic online research but is relatively straightforward. Simply trawl the websites of your preferred resorts and click on anything that might offer the promise of the availability of a celebrated film or sports star. Such people, particularly in the USA, regularly make themselves available to ski resorts as 'ambassadors' for promotional purposes. In return they get handsome remuneration, a free season's lift pass and the pleasure of skiing with fully qualified bluffers.

If you happen to be carrying your 35mm movie camera at the time, you won't have to worry about finding the slebs – especially when you have previously informed the resort that you're looking for someone to play a cameo role in a big-budget ski flick. The luvvies will sniff you out quicker than a mountain-rescue dog.

Skiers on chairlifts take an unhealthy
interest in skiers beneath them
and actually urge them to fall over.

LIFTS AND QUEUES

There is a basic Newtonian logic to skiing: you have to go up before you can ski down. Going up involves a variety of forms. Take careful note of each because some knowledge of ski lifts is essential for all-round dissembling.

CABLE CARS

Called *téléphérique*, *seilbahn* or *funivia* in the Alps, and 'trams' in the USA, the cable car has queues at both ends and should be avoided by claustrophobics. They should also be avoided early and late in the day by anyone with an aversion to body odour, boiled eggs, flatulence, aftershave, acne and intimate contact with strangers.

They are at their most crowded first thing in the morning. Often they are also very busy last thing in the afternoon when there is either no other way to the bottom, no snow or people just can't be bothered to ski anymore. On these occasions they are even more of an olfactory endurance test than in the morning.

Experienced skiers like to demonstrate their superior

knowledge by being first or last in and standing by the door (there are usually doors on both sides). This supposedly gives them a 50% chance of getting off first. Don't believe a word of it. Only one door opens at a time – and it's always the one furthest away from you.

FUNICULARS AND MOUNTAIN RAILWAYS

Funiculars are dependent on cables to pull one up while another is coming down. They differ from cable cars in so far as they are either on the ground or under the ground. This makes them popular with skiers who don't care to be dangled in the air.

Traditionalists say that nothing beats the old 'cog' and 'rack-and-pinion' mountain railways in Switzerland, which go up impossible gradients painfully slowly. The steepest rack railway in the world is up Mount Pilatus near Lucerne, but you are advised not to talk too authoritatively about the skiing at the top. There isn't any.

GONDOLAS

Gondolas are probably the most comfortable and convenient form of mountain transport. As with chairs, skiers are always guaranteed a seat – but they differ from chairs in that skiers don't die of exposure on the way.

Gondolas have a man in a stripy T-shirt on board singing 'O Sole Mio', but that's only in Venice. On mountains they have up to six skiers staring silently out of the window and pretending that the others aren't there – unless they're all friends with each other, or Americans. In the

USA gondolas are called 'bubbles' because they are shaped like them. You should state confidently that gondolas are the best form of mountain lift. Only environmentalists will disagree.

CHAIRLIFTS

Chairs range from ancient one-seaters to 'high-speed detachable quads' (four to six seats in a row, although they can go up to eight). Many skiers are understandably worried by the 'detachable' bit, but that has something to do with a device for temporarily detaching them from the cable so that skiers can get on and off easily. Gondolas have these as well. Despite this thoughtfulness, all chairs are designed to smack into the back of your legs just above the boot and cause you to squawk involuntarily and fall backwards onto the seat.

You are required to keep your skis on for the duration of the journey. This is largely academic because they always come off when you collide with your fellow passengers in the scramble to get off. Fight tooth and nail for the outside seat and ski off at an acute angle at the top to avoid trouble. Avoid getting on chairlifts with Americans (difficult in the USA) because they always tell you their life story. When the lift gets stuck, there's no escape.

T-BARS

Unquestionably the most irksome form of transport ever devised, T-bars first made a simultaneous appearance in Zürs in Austria and Davos in Switzerland. The Austrians and Swiss must never be forgiven for their folly.

T-bars are shaped like an upside-down letter 'T'. They tow two skiers – each with one half of the crossbar wedged into some part of their lower anatomy. No two skiers are ever the same size, which renders balance virtually impossible and ensures that all four skis will veer off in different directions.

There is one absolute certainty about T-bars. When they finally eject you, they will do so in the most difficult terrain on the mountain. And that's no place to be with a stranger when it's your fault you both fell off.

BUTTON LIFTS

Button lifts are better than T-bars because they take only one person at a time, and the soup-plate-sized 'button' between the legs is easier to keep in place. Beginners will quickly learn not to sit down on the soup plates ('platters' in the USA, *pomas* in the Alps). They present different problems for men and women. Women should be wary of button-lift attendants with a glint in the eye, which invariably means that they will find a hand between the button and their buttocks.

Men should be wary for the same reason but should also be prepared for the pole to be yanked smartly upwards into their gonads. For some reason this provides lift attendants with considerable amusement. Males should grit their teeth and allow their eyes to water without saying a word.

LIFT PASSES/ATTENDANTS

Lift passes (tickets in the USA) are the accepted way of paying for the lift. In many resorts the passes are now computer coded, requiring them to be fed into a machine or passed by a scanner. These rarely work, necessitating a bad-tempered lift attendant to come out of his hut and shout at you. This usually has the effect of rousing the 200-strong queue behind to shout at you as well. Try to maintain a dignified silence in these circumstances.

When a T-bar finally ejects you, it will do so in the most difficult terrain on the mountain.

Never wear your pass on elastic around your neck. One of the many ways lift attendants amuse themselves is by extending the elastic to its full length and catapulting the pass back into your eye (particularly true of US 'lifties' who frequently read tickets by a hand-held scanner).

It's as well to be aware of certain fundamental axioms about different countries' lift systems and their attendants:

Switzerland Like their trains – fast, safe, efficient, often ingeniously tunnelled. Not always ingeniously linked. Attendants smart, brusque and stony-faced. They're wondering why, if all Swiss are supposed to be rich, they aren't.

France Unnecessarily overdeveloped to the point of irresponsibility. De Gaulle's fault. Extraordinarily convenient, often leaving within inches of one's front door. Cleverly linked. Attendants have a serious attitude problem.

Austria Usually involve long walks out of town. This keeps towns and villages nice and unspoilt, but is tough on the feet. Methodical, worthy, reliable. Reputed to be bought second-hand from the Swiss. Too many T-bars. Attendants usually Australian.

Italy Deeply suspect. Mussolini's fault. Extraordinarily ambitious and high-tech and therefore unreliable; or primitive and therefore unreliable. Much of the superstructure reputed to be bought third-hand from the Austrians. Attendants irrepressibly cheerful and utterly unreliable. Hands everywhere.

Eastern Europe Antiquated, slow and dodgy. Lenin's fault. Reputed to be bought fourth-hand from the Italians. Cable car in Poland needs to be booked a month in advance. Attendants charming, helpful; keen to sell you caviar and currency.

USA Fast and comfortable, but too dependent on chairs. Not many chairs have safety bars. Not always too cleverly linked. Attendants greet you like old friends. Always say, 'How's it goin'?' followed by, 'Have a good one.' It is sometimes tempting to insert a ski pole where the sun don't shine.

QUEUE ETIQUETTE

The British, having invented them, know all about queues. The majority of continental Europeans do not have the same sense of fair play and act as if queues don't exist. This is an important point to note because the right response to queue-barging is not to foam conspicuously at the mouth but to shake the head with an air of weary resignation. This proves to your companions that you have been in this situation many times before and accept that confrontation is not the answer.

If you are feeling particularly bold you can make great play of the queue-barger's churlishness by exclaiming in a loud voice: 'Stand back. This person is in a hurry. Let him/her through because clearly he/she has something very important to do.' It won't make any difference but you'll feel a lot better. Queue-bargers do not understand sarcasm because they are not very intelligent. Generally they have very low foreheads and very long arms. They tend to be French, German or, increasingly, Russian – in which case they will almost certainly be drunk. Queue-bargers in Europe are never American. Americans will stand aside for hours at a time, waiting for a lift attendant to tell them it's their turn.

If a queue-barger is behaving so badly that something simply has to be done, follow him or her very closely until you are both deep in the core of the heaving scrum. Position the point of your pole carefully over one of their binding releases and press downwards. If you have the opportunity, release both. The result, when they push forward towards the lift, is invariably satisfying. Even if they get on the tow bar or chair, the ski will almost certainly fall off – and nobody looks too smart with just one ski on.

♛

Nobody looks too
smart with just one ski on.

If, in the scrum, the same thing should happen to you, there is regrettably very little you can do to keep your dignity intact. The only slim chance of coming through it with some credit is to pretend that you did it on purpose, but this calls for bluffing skills of the highest magnitude and requires a prolonged amount of acrobatic clowning – a type of slapstick humour that continental Europeans are unaccountably partial to. If you can carry it off successfully, you may even be able to supplement your holiday budget by passing around your hat. Do not, however, expect too much from the Germans. Most of them will have taken advantage of the diversion to move a hundred yards ahead.

SKIING UNDER CHAIRLIFTS

The best advice about skiing under chairlifts is: don't. Skiers on chairlifts take an unhealthy interest in skiers beneath them and actually urge them to fall over. Often you will fall over because you will be aware of being closely watched and therefore be keen to impress.

Never, ever try to impress people on a chairlift. Even if you succeed in skiing passably well, your efforts will be sneeringly dismissed as showing off. If you fall over, you will earn about as much sympathy as a fillet steak could reasonably expect from a Rottweiler.

If you do find yourself skiing under a chairlift, wait until someone worse than you comes by. Ski as close to them as prudence allows and, if you think you can get away with it, pretend that you are teaching them.

Après-ski describes that convivial period at the end of the day when skiers get together, have a few drinks and then lie disgracefully about their skiing exploits.

SURVIVING

AVALANCHES

The thing you really need to know about avalanches is that they aren't called the 'white death' for nothing. Having brought up the subject, sooner or later someone will ask you if you have been caught in one. If your audience is not cooperating, say something rhetorical like: 'Believe me. An avalanche is no laughing matter. I…no, perhaps it's better left unsaid.'

When pressed, pause, and gaze stoically into the distance. If you can manage it without dribbling, allow your bottom lip to quiver slightly. After a suitably pregnant silence, say softly: 'It's not easy to talk about.' This is true, of course, because you know absolutely nothing about it. Follow this by saying enigmatically: 'Did you know that an airborne powder snow avalanche can travel at speeds of up to 190 miles per hour? That's not too easy to keep ahead of – even for me.'

If this doesn't have them marvelling, continue with: 'A block of wet snow three feet square weighs about three-quarters of a ton. Imagine the weight of something the size of a football pitch coming down the mountain after you.' As you say this, rub your thigh bone ruminatively and resolutely refuse to take the matter further. If you really want to push your luck, say: 'I was one of the lucky ones. But I can never ski the Widowmaker again.'

There are two basic forms of avalanche that you might want to pretend to know about: loose snow and slab avalanches. Neither is much fun. If you hear an avalanche (interesting paralysing effect) you will usually be safe in saying: 'Sounds like a slab.' If, on the other hand, there has recently been a fresh 'dump' of snow and you're not sure what sort it is, try: 'Sounds like an avalanche,' and get down the mountain as quickly as possible.

A loose snow avalanche can be caused by the weight of a heavy fall of new 'powder' snow on a very steep slope, or by 'wet' snow that has thawed and not 'bonded' properly with a fresh fall. A slab avalanche (the most common kind) happens when a fracture line breaks and releases a huge amount of snow in blocks in a sort of domino effect. It is usually caused by wind, and not the sort you will be short of if it hits you.

GLACIERS

At some stage you will need to pretend that you know something about glaciers. Glaciers are moving rivers of ice that pulverise everything in their path. Fortunately their progress is generally slow – no more than an inch or two a day so that even the British Olympic ski team can keep ahead of them, but in Alaska and Iceland they can steam along at up to 15 feet an hour.

Glaciers start very high up the mountain above the permanent snow line and are 'fed' by the permanent 'snow fields'. They can be skied on with minimal risk if your guide (essential precaution) knows where the crevasses are. This is all you really need to know about glaciers apart from certain key words such as 'seracs' (pinnacles of ice that form eye-catching sculptures), 'moraines' (the debris of crushed stone at the glacier's sides and end) and 'snout' (the front end). Familiarity with these terms will ensure instant respect from all who have the pleasure of listening to you.

For the more ghoulish, there are stories about perfectly preserved mountaineers and skiers being disgorged by glaciers many years after their deaths. How this is supposed to happen if glaciers can reduce boulders to dust, nobody has satisfactorily explained. But it makes a good story.

CREVASSES

Never claim to have fallen into a crevasse. The chances of getting out alive are slim, so people will be disinclined to believe you; and the reasons for falling into the icy fissure in the first place have more to do with negligence than fortitude. In any discussion about crevasses, the best approach is to pretend that you risked your life rescuing some other poor fool who skied too close to one. So you will need to know what a crevasse is. They are big holes in a glacier caused by glacial movement and subsequent fractures in the ice. They are generally very deep (up to 200 feet) and always dangerous. They can also be difficult to spot because their 'lips' are often concealed by snow. This means that, when snow collapses beneath a skier's weight, the crevasse has a disturbing tendency to show its true contours rather suddenly – sucking anybody standing on top into its frozen depths.

Hope of rescue is often futile because if the fall doesn't kill you, the intense cold probably will. Furthermore, most professional rescuers have a healthy respect for crevasses and prefer to stay a safe distance away.

<hr>

♛

> Hope of rescue from a crevasse is often futile because if the fall doesn't kill you, the intense cold probably will.

<hr>

If, however, you are determined to push your deceptive powers to the limit, you should explain that the victim was fortunate enough to land on a 'snow bridge'. This is a build-up of hard snow spanning the crevasse which is usually flimsy and not to be relied on, so even the most shameless bluffer should not claim to have dropped fearlessly onto it, skis clamped firmly between teeth. Waffle instead about ropes and crampons and painstaking precautions and first aid. With any luck your audience will have fallen asleep before they see through you.

COULOIRS

'Couloir' is the French word for corridor. These are very steep and narrow sections of terrain, almost exclusively found off-piste, that get steeper and narrower as you pick up speed. On either side are jagged walls of ice and rock, and they usually have an abrupt dog-leg at the end which requires a braking, scraping, screaming, near-impossible 90-degree turn.

If anybody has the temerity to ask you whether you have skied a particularly notorious couloir (which, naturally, you will never have been anywhere near), wave a dismissive hand and say that you're 'not interested in motorways' (wide, cruising slopes). If they persist, say: 'Look, unless it's "Body Bag", forget it.'

SNOWSTORMS

Also known as 'white-outs'. Cold, merciless and unpredictable, they can reduce visibility to the end of your nose. When they occur, the best course is to follow your nose to the nearest mountain restaurant and wait until it blows over. With luck it won't and you can stay in the restaurant all night, later telling your friends that you had to dig a snowhole and survive for 10 hours in freezing temperatures. White-outs usually occur when you are stuck on a chairlift.

BEING STUCK ON A CHAIRLIFT

This is one of the coldest and most trying events you can experience. It is made marginally worse by being on the windward side or next to a garrulous American. Ways of passing the time include snapping off your frozen fingers and throwing them at lift attendants dithering about below.

FROZEN FINGERS

The time-honoured way of dealing with frozen fingers is to point them downwards and shake them vigorously to keep the blood flowing. Amazingly, it works.

SNOW CANNONS

These are artificial snow-making machines used by resorts with a dodgy snow record to cover a couple of square yards of barren, rocky piste. How the snow is actually 'made' is anybody's guess, but it's supposed to have something to do with temperature, water pressure, underground reservoirs and so on.

What is important is knowing where they are likely to be sited. Rather like piste bashers, snow cannons lurk round corners waiting for unsuspecting skiers to arrive before starting up. There is no recommended course to adopt when finding yourself skiing into a dense cloud of artificial snow. We suggest you close your eyes and pray.

APRÈS-SKI

Surviving après-ski is one of the most important parts of the skier's Survival Code. The term was invented by the French to describe that convivial period at the end of the day when skiers get together, have a few drinks and then lie disgracefully about their skiing exploits. Unaccountably, the French then effectively abolished après-ski by building hideous, Stalinist-style prison camps all over the French Alps, thereby making it virtually impossible for anyone to enjoy anything. There are a few bars left in some of the concrete blocks, but staff have been so brutalised by their environment that they can rarely muster more than a snarl.

Where après-ski still thrives – notably Austria, Canada and Italy – there are certain basic rules to observe:

- Always ensure that one of your party remains sober enough to show the rest of you the way home.

- Never urinate against a lamp post in freezing conditions (unless someone is prepared to detach you).

- Avoid excessive intake of glühwein (a curious alcoholic cough mixture once described by a ski writer as 'a useful adhesive for securing a hairpiece').

MOUNTAIN RESTAURANTS

Here, everything costs up to three times as much as in the resort. A useful formula for calculating the percentage increase is: 50% for every 1,000 feet in altitude.

The best mountain restaurants are easily identified by the sight of British, French, Germans and Italians engaged in pitched battles for tables and chairs on the sun terraces. Alliances are not always split on wartime lines, but you should expect the Germans to win (having previously bribed the restaurant staff to intervene on their behalf).

Mountain restaurants are also identifiable by large signs that read 'NO DRINK – NO WC'. Because there is never anywhere else to relieve yourself on the mountain, the cost of queuing to use the restaurant's only lavatory (in France, a hole in the floor) can be as much as the price of a Pschitt (*see* Glossary).

ALTITUDE

Surviving the effects of increased altitude is relatively straightforward if you don't exert yourself. But since a skiing holiday is likely to be the only time of the year that you actually do exert yourself, you need to be prepared for it. If you have ever witnessed a grounded fish gasping on a river bank, you will have some idea of what to expect at the end of your first mogul field. Sometimes it can be that bad just getting out of bed. This is especially true of the USA, where many Colorado resorts are located at about 9,000 feet.

Altitude sickness is a common complaint among those who don't want to admit that they are chronically unfit. But there are some advantages. For example, it doesn't require much alcohol to become completely incapacitated. This can result in significant savings. Furthermore (and more importantly) hangovers are for some reason much more bearable.

There are two useful facts to have in store for altitude conversations:

1. Above 1,500 metres (4,900 feet) it takes twice as long to boil an egg.

2. Ultraviolet (UV) intensity increases by up to 20% for every 1,500 metres of altitude, and snow reflects up to 85% UV radiation (a good reason for reapplying your total sunblock).

BLOOD WAGONS

This is the cheerful name given to canvas hammocks slung between two wild-eyed stretcher-bearers on skis. Those who have taken this means of downhill transport (usually due to injury) report that nine times out of 10 they would instead prefer to suffer the injury again.

Blood-wagon skiers (one at the front, one at the back, or side by side if the back one is faster) are usually frustrated Olympic downhill skiers. Like their heroes, they aim, point, gather speed and refuse to turn – even for rocks. Their sole objective is to cause maximum discomfort to the crippled passenger. They are remarkably proficient at their job.

INJURIES

The most important thing to remember about ski-oriented injuries is that they should be described with lurid dispassion. An entirely imaginary shard of bone that once pierced your ski trousers can be described in the most gory detail and at length – so long as the description is casually qualified by: 'I'd just bought the bloody things as well.'

There are certain basic injuries that every skier should claim to have suffered. The 'twisted knee' is perhaps the most common. 50% of snow-skiing injuries involve the leg, and half of these involve the knee. To describe your real or imagined injury as a mere 'twist' is to waste a glorious opportunity for some shameless bluffing. A 'partial rupture of the anterior cruciate ligament' is what should be said instead. Only orthopaedic surgeons know what this means, if anything, so unless your audience is comprised of genuine bone boffins, you should be on safe ground. If pressed for further details, gabble about white fibrous tissues, inflammation, femurs, tibias and how you suffered it by landing heavily on a rock to avoid a small child. 'Sudden deceleration,' you will say sadly, 'it always gets the old cruciate.'

If your injury is minor, resist the temptation to play it up too much. This will not only tempt fate but you are bound to forget to limp at a crucial moment. The best course is to say: 'I think I got away with it – this time.' If, on the other hand (heaven forbid), it is major, play it up with the crashing accompaniment of a full symphony orchestra. The right approach is to say: 'It'll hurt like hell, but I'm not going to let that mountain defeat me.' Tears will spring to your audience's eyes and, with luck, yours as well, followed by widespread admiration for being such a stalwart.

Other popular injuries are in the shoulder region. If you happen to land on the point of your shoulder, you will not need to bluff; the pain – or the memory of it – will be plain for all to see. But if you insist on pressing your luck, choose to have dislocated it in a spectacular crash, occasioned by consideration for the inexperienced. There is a very useful word to remember in this context: 'Damned thing popped out. I was dragging my knuckles around the mountain like an orangutan until a passing pisteur (*see* Ski Types) popped it back in.' 'Popping', therefore, is a vital part of any injured skier's vocabulary. It has the distinct advantage of suggesting pluck and fortitude in the face of adversity, and is guaranteed to turn any listener faint.

There is a useful piece of injury-suggestive equipment that you might consider acquiring – especially when you know that your lack of skiing ability is about to be exposed: invest in a high-tech surgical knee brace. This makes it impossible to ski with any degree of style, and also says a great deal about your extraordinary courage for skiing at all. If you want to look particularly stoical, invest in two – even if this does have the effect of making you walk like John Wayne.

WHAT INJURIES NOT TO HAVE

A bruised bottom, no matter how severe, is always a cause for mirth. Worse still, it suggests that you can't ski properly. Sprained thumbs and ingrowing toenails are also to be avoided. They hurt like hell, keep you awake at night, make you very bad-tempered and earn you no sympathy whatsoever.

It will be tempting to maintain
that you have never needed a lesson in
your life. This is ill-advised, not least
because it will lay you open to the
entirely legitimate retort: 'Yes, it shows.'

TECHNIQUE

The first thing you need to appreciate is that no amount of reading about skiing will teach you how to look good on skis. One solution is to steer well clear of any situation where you might have to prove how advanced your 'technique' is to the people you've been bluffing. This will be difficult, not least because it means that you won't be able to ski with your friends (the most likely victims of your delusions).

A more expedient solution is to know something about the theory even if you haven't a clue how to put it into practice. This will ensure that you can talk a good bit about skiing – despite the fact that you spend conspicuously more time on your back than on your skis. You could always resort to our suggested catalogue of excuses (*see* Injuries, Equipment, Conditions, etc.) to explain why.

THE THEORY

The basic theory of skiing technique is that once you have conquered your fear of the 'fall line', you have essentially cracked the secret of how to ski. After that it is just a matter of refining your technique – i.e., 'looking good'. Looking good is the whole point of technique, although purists will tell you that 'control' is what it's all about.

Control is something that will be alien to most ski bluffers. Nonetheless, you must make stern and responsible noises about how vital it is for safe and effective skiing, and secretly strive to attain it. Exactly why it's so vital will become clear when you need to stop, or take evasive action – suddenly. This happens quite a lot.

The fall line is the steepest, and therefore the quickest, way down a slope. In other words, if you were not planning on turning at any stage, this would be the route your skis would take you (assuming that you were still attached to them). Instructors and instruction books will tell you that fall lines have nothing to do with falling over. In that case, you might well ask, 'Why are they called fall lines?'

Being told not to be frightened of the fall line is akin to being told not to worry when you fall out of a light aircraft some distance above the ground. The shortest distance between the aircraft door and the ground is also called a fall line, because that is the way you will fall. Your instinctive reaction when first looking down a fall line on a mountain will be to imagine the 'no-parachute' scenario – and, therefore, to wish to give vent to your fear. Resist this impulse at all costs, especially if you have an audience.

There are ways of coping with the fall line. To start with, there is:

THE SNOWPLOUGH

This is not a heavy-duty farm implement but a method of controlling your rate of descent by forming your skis into a V-shaped wedge, with the tips forming a narrow head and the tails as wide apart as you can get them. The wider apart the tails, the slower you go – in theory.

If it is a particularly steep fall line, you might yell with false bravado, 'See you in hell,' before setting off.

Unfortunately, snowploughs are not very effective on steep fall lines. They also have the singular disadvantage of suggesting to the world that you can't ski. It will be necessary, therefore, to adopt another technique for coping, for example:

SCHUSSING

A 'schuss' is popular with those skiers with a 'let's-melt-mountain' mentality. It involves keeping the skis together, aiming the tips down the fall line and hoping for the best. If it is a particularly steep fall line, you might yell with false bravado, 'See you in hell,' before setting off. Sometimes (most of the time) it is difficult to stop on a schuss. It is therefore important to determine whether or not there is a reasonably flattish bit at the bottom (known as a 'run-out'). If there isn't, think twice before going.

There is a special position to adopt in the schuss. It's a sort of crouch called a 'tuck' or an 'egg', where you bend down over the skis with your bottom in the air, your poles tucked into your armpits. It looks absurd and it causes a peculiarly painful sensation in your thigh muscles. There must be good reason for doing it, like minimal wind resistance, but the real reason probably has more to do with the fact that you will be that much closer to the ground when you fall over.

EDGING

'Edging' is the term given to the practice of pressing the metal edges of your skis into the snow. If you don't want to go straight down the fall line, you can stand at right angles to it with both your skis across the slope and their 'uphill' edges 'biting' into it. If they don't bite properly you will find yourself embarked on another method – 'side slipping' (see page 66). If they do bite properly, you will remain stationary – even (one is assured) on near-vertical slopes. Edging is therefore a useful technique to acquire and to be familiar with, as in: 'Good to see your edging's coming along,' or: 'Experts always ski on their edges' (except, of course, when they're schussing).

Having established the point of edges, the next stage is to see what happens when you change your right-angle position by a couple of degrees. If you point the tips of the properly edged skis uphill you will slide backwards; if you point them downhill you will slide forwards. The general idea, if you want to move, is to point them downhill.

As yet there is no variant of the sport called 'skiing backwards' – unless you count freestyle.

TRAVERSING

The actual movement of crossing a slope like this is called a 'traverse'. In theory it describes any manoeuvre where your skis follow any straight line other than the fall line. Like edging, it is a useful technique to acquire. Ideally, you should be edging all the time that you are traversing. It is the quickest way to get down the mountain (apart from rolling).

At some stage your traverse will have to come to an end, otherwise you will traverse straight over a cliff or into a tree. The means of doing so is called:

TURNING

Turning is fundamental to skiing, although many skiers – notably blood-wagon bearers, pigs-on-planks (*see* Ski Types) and novices – disagree. A normal descent, unless it is a schuss, is a series of 'linked' turns. Or should be. Note that you never simply turn; you always 'carve' a turn. Carving a turn takes many different forms:

The snowplough turn

On reflection, snowplough turns are rarely 'carved'; they are ploughed. The idea is that you put more weight on one ski than the other in the snowplough position and, miraculously, you turn in the opposite direction to the weighted ski. Exactly why this happens need not concern you. Just declare 'weighting' to be the basis of all turning technique.

The stem turn

This is a snowplough turn that starts and finishes with the skis together in a normal traverse position. You just have to remember to open or 'stem' them at the right moment, otherwise you might skip a lesson or two and do a 'parallel' turn by mistake. If you do manage to do a parallel turn by mistake, try to remember how you did it.

The stem christie

This takes its name from 'Christiania', which is what Oslo used to be called and where the turn was invented. Essentially, it is a speeded-up stem turn with – and this is the tricky bit – the skis together when you reach the fall line. This involves split-second weight transference and a lot of 'sinking down', 'springing up' and 'angulation' to come out of the fall line. If you haven't quite mastered it, you 'hit' the fall line and don't come out of it. Then you find yourself yelping and doing an involuntary schuss.

The parallel turn

'Skiing parallel' used to describe the practice of keeping your skis glued together throughout the entire turn. The few who managed to achieve this unlikely feat after years of determined endeavour are now told that the skis should be hip-width apart instead of stuck together. This is conclusive proof of a worldwide conspiracy among ski instructors to redefine technique whenever they feel like it, thus ensuring a constant supply of work.

The jet turn

The 'jet' turn sounds terrific and looks terrific. In essence it's a parallel turn with the skier sitting back – which is exactly what you are not supposed to do. It involves 'checking', 'anticipating', 'sinking', 'unweighting', 'braking' and 'carving'. All you have to remember is to do all these things in the space of about one-hundredth of a second. Simple, really.

The compression turn

Another name for colliding with a mogul and discovering that your knees have been relocated two feet above your head. The technique necessitates appropriate 'absorption' of the bump. It was invented by the French, who insist on calling it an *avalement* turn. *Avalement* means 'swallow', which is what you may do with your knees while attempting to execute this manoeuvre.

The wedel turn

The art of linking short parallel turns in a rhythmic up-down bouncing motion. The concept is that one turn flows directly into another in a rapid 'wagging' motion, with the upper body facing downhill all the time. 'Wedeling' comes from the German word *wedeln* (to wag) and has nothing to do with ski journalists wheedling free meals.

The jump turn

One that comes in handy on very steep slopes and in deep, heavy snow. Often initiated from a stationary position, it requires both skis to turn in mid-air and face the opposite direction. If the tips cross in mid-execution, you may well engage in interesting acrobatics for the remainder of your descent.

The carving turn

Turns on carving skis require a different technique, but no one (least of all instructors) can agree what it is. Thus you will hear lots of conflicting advice about 'rolling your ankles', 'even-weighting' and 'following your shoulders'. Ignore it all. Carving skis make whatever turn they like.

Side slipping

Perhaps the most effective technique of all for dealing with the fall line, especially for those who prefer not to schuss or turn. It involves a mixture of edging and 'flattening' the skis. When both skis are flattened together, they will slide sideways downhill until the edges are 'reset'. For some unaccountable reason, when you reach the bottom in safety, friends gather around and chant 'chicken'. This is most unfair and confers a completely undeserved stigma on a perfectly valid means of descent.

STOPPING

This is an oft-neglected technique that can involve a great deal of buttock-contact with the mountainside. There are other ways of executing a stop manoeuvre, like braking with your edges and pointing your ski-tips uphill, but nothing really beats the buttock routine for all-round style and effectiveness.

PREPARATION

This is something that skiers are supposed to do assiduously for three or more months before their holiday. It is also called 'exercise' or 'getting fit'. In reality, most skiers talk about it a lot but avoid doing anything about it with a determination that is quite uncharacteristic. A standard excuse is that you 'don't want to aggravate your old ligament injury'.

Then there are lessons. It will be tempting to maintain that you have never needed a lesson in your life. This is ill-advised, not least because it will lay you open to the entirely legitimate retort: 'Yes, it shows.' Instead, candidly admit that you had a lesson in the early days – just to learn the basics. Nobody need ever know that learning the basics took you up to 10 weeks.

At ski school you will learn how to join up to 30 other people in following an instructor down a slope. The fact that 29 of them can't see what the instructor is doing is irrelevant. Ski school is a good way of meeting people, discovering (hopefully) that there are some worse than you, and confirming that few instructors speak intelligible English. Don't be surprised at being referred to as 'imbécile', 'idiot', 'dummkopf' or 'buffone' – terms of affection in French, Scottish, German and Italian – when you admit to some confusion about what you are supposed to do. Speed of comprehension depends on whether you have private or group lessons. Reckon on one private lesson being worth about five group lessons. Take full advantage of this opportunity to learn the following basics: how to stand, how to get up, how to turn and how to stop. This is all you really need to know apart from tips to help you cope with the following conditions:

ICE

There is no known technique for handling ice on the piste, and normal skiing procedures like edging have little effect. When most skiers encounter ice, they have a panic attack, try to turn and then perform a 'splits' routine. You will, of course, know better than to turn – you won't be on the slope in the first place. The worst sort of ice is 'boilerplate' (*see* Glossary).

POWDER

This is the nice, ungroomed, fluffy stuff you find off-piste – a place that bluffers talk about incessantly but where they rarely venture. All enthusiasts need to know is that 'powder skiing' is the next best thing to sex. Key words include 'exhilarating', 'deep', 'floating', 'virgin' and 'serpent trails'. The latter are what you will claim to have left behind you in 'virgin powder'. The fact that your trail will look more like you've been dragging a fir tree should never be mentioned.

When the question of how to do it comes up, as it will, you need to know that a different technique is required. All you have to say is, 'It's all in the weighting,' and promptly change the subject.

Never admit to skiing on 'fat boys' – extra-wide skis that bounce along on the surface of the snow and make it possible for even the perpendicularly challenged to powder ski. Instead, you should insist that 'fat skiing' is cheating and potentially calamitous for purists – then hire a pair as soon as you can.

If you are imprudent enough to attempt powder skiing on conventional equipment, remember one vital piece of advice. To save time looking for your skis in three feet of snow it's a good idea to carry a pair of 'powder straps' – lengths of elastic that attach skis to boots and strangle you in the avalanche you have just triggered. Even if you never have cause to use them, you can throw them casually on to the table in mountain restaurants and bars when you're sure someone is looking.

A big fall of new snow is called a 'dump'. If you call it anything else you reveal gross inexperience.

SNOWCRAFT

Easy familiarity with different forms of snow is an extremely useful bluffing device. Indeed, most skiers will be surprised to know that there is more than one type.

What 'sort' of snow it may be is determined by a number of factors including temperature, amount of water in the atmosphere, wind speed at the time of the snowfall and the changes it undergoes once it has landed. You can impress people hugely by 'examining' it and pronouncing on your findings. The snowball test is crucial here. You don't have to know what it is supposed to prove but it has something to do with 'fusion'. If you can make a nice compact snowball, the snow is likely to be old. If it won't fuse at all, it's probably new. Of course, you could tell whether it's old or new by looking out of the window to see if it is snowing. But that's not the point. The point is that its 'age' says a lot about how it will ski and whether it is likely to avalanche. All snow can avalanche.

A big fall of new snow is called a 'dump'. If you call it anything else you reveal gross inexperience. If that should happen, you will need to gabble at length about:

Hard-pack Oldish powder snow compressed into a hard, beaten surface by a piste-basher.

Powder snow Fresh snow that hasn't begun to melt. It is dry, loose and impossible to make into snowballs. It squeaks when you walk on it and three or four inches of it on a 'firm base' is every skier's dream.

Spring snow Powder that has begun to thaw but is refrozen overnight into hard, granular particles. Usually only found early in the morning late in the season. Also known as 'corn' snow. Pretend to have risen at dawn 'to look for it' (but remember only to search on south-facing slopes). It is the holy grail of snow until it warms up and turns into 'slush'.

Crust An icy layer on top of powder, found off-piste. If thin and easily broken, it is said to be not too difficult. If thick and only breaks on turns, it's 'breakable crust', one of the least attractive surfaces to ski on. Your ski will happily surge on ahead in the soft snow beneath but your boot will have to act like a polar ice-breaker. For instant credibility, claim that it causes you no real problems.

Porridge, mashed potato or Sierra cement Thick, sticky, old snow in an advanced state of decay. Difficult to turn on. Has a tendency to gather at the bottom of runs or any other place where large crowds congregate to watch the carnage.

VARIATIONS

CROSS-COUNTRY

The oldest form of skiing, variously known as 'Nordic' because the Nords invented it, *langlauf* in German, *ski de fond* in French and *sci di fondo* in Italian. Involving the use of a long, thin, curly ski, it feels similar to a fast walk with strips of fettuccine attached to your feet. It has little in common with downhill skiing, in which excessive expertise may only be a hindrance. Bluffers will therefore enjoy a distinct advantage in mastering cross-country skiing.

Other points to note include the fact that you must wear a skin-tight, very shiny body stocking to look the part and, best of all – if you should happen to take part in an event – you are expected to fall over at the finish line in a state of total exhaustion.

UPHILL

Otherwise known as ski touring or ski mountaineering, this was originally designed for masochists, members of the SAS (same thing) and French Army conscripts (poor sods). It requires a level of physical fitness close to that expected of a double-marathon runner. It involves climbing up mountains with your skis on for hours on end – a feat only made possible by special bindings that allow the heel to lift out of the heel unit, and 'skins' that are attached to the soles of the skis to prevent them sliding backwards. Skins used to be made out of seal hides but are now made from something synthetic and prickly. Ski tourers like staying in remote mountain refuges and bluffing to each other that they're not close to death from excessive physical exertion.

MONOSKIING

This is neither skiing on your own because you can't allow your friends to see how inept you are, nor skiing on one ski because the other has fallen off. The term is used to cover the practice of skiing on a single broad ski with a dual binding that accommodates both feet side by side. Monoskiers tend to plant their poles more viciously than duo-skiers; it's the only way that they can keep their balance. Sadly, it is now almost extinct.

SNOWBOARDING

Also known as 'surfing' or 'shredding', this is a cross between wave-surfing and monoskiing – but without poles or sharks. Snowboards always have 'turbo' written on them somewhere and travel at speeds upwards of Mach 2. Snowboarders, or 'riders' (sometimes known as 'gays-on-trays'), usually have long hair, sometimes in fetching ponytails, and shout things like 'Awesome, dude!' when they crash into you. This is one example of a completely impenetrable language that all skiers will be required to learn. Within the next decade it is estimated that snowboarders will outnumber skiers. That's because it's easier to learn. Incidentally, they have been known to describe skiers as 'pricks-on-sticks'.

KITE SKIING

Kite skiers (also known as snowkiters) rely on large kites and wind, rather than poles and gravity, for propulsion. They like being tugged along on skis across large, flat, open spaces like frozen lakes, but sometimes you can see them trying to ski uphill to save buying a lift pass. This can be unexpectedly entertaining, especially when they catch a sudden gust of wind and achieve an unexpected degree of uplift. The sport is relatively new, and the jury is still out on whether it will take off.

SNOWBLADES/SKIBOARDS

These oddly truncated, highly manoeuvrable skis – typically no more than 90cm long – are essentially the same but manufacturers still can't decide what to call them. In the early 1960s their predecessors were imaginatively known as 'short skis' and were popular with French and US ski schools because they were easier to control. Being seen around a resort with them was therefore akin to having an 'L' plate on your back, and an invitation for every skier to race up behind you at speed screaming, 'Outta my way, butthead!' or 'Dégage, crétin!' Oddly enough, they didn't catch on.

They enjoyed a brief reincarnation as 'Bigfeet' – even shorter skis, with wider tips and 'toes' amusingly painted on them. Now they are undergoing a serious renaissance because it takes about 30 seconds to learn how to use them. Traditional skiers hate them because it has taken them about 30 years to reach the same standard. The idea is that short skis are easier to control. This is generally true except in a schuss when they slide all over the place.

SKI/SNOW BIKES

Ludicrous contraptions that are essentially bicycles with skis instead of wheels and 'pegs' instead of pedals. Difficult to control, and even more difficult to look cool on. Skiers should give them a wide berth (even wider than for snowboarders).

TELEMARKING

A cross between cross-country and downhill skiing, it involves skiing downhill on cross-country skis. This requires a completely different turning technique, involving going down on one knee, rather like a medieval knight. It takes its name from the Norwegian province of Telemark where it was invented. Colorado exponents of the art are known as 'raisin pickers'.

FREESTYLE SKIING

Something few skiers do on purpose, it involves performing somersaults, aerobatics, spins, splits, landing on your head – all manoeuvres the bluffer can expect to perform in a typical day on the piste. Freestyle skiers may have skis called 'twin tips', with upturned rounded tips at both ends, so that they can ski backwards and show off even more.

HELI-SKIING

You know the feeling when you alight onto that squeaky powder, hunched under the clattering rotor blades of a chopper, hands clamped over your ears, knees shaking in anticipation of a couple of vertical miles of creamy untracked snow, whistling *The Ride of the Valkyries* as you begin to skim over those seductively sparkling mountaintops as the world lies at your feet? No, of course you don't. But that's not the point.

♛

True ski bluffers wouldn't dream of admitting that they have never been heli-skiing.

You've been there in your imagination, and that's what counts. True ski bluffers wouldn't dream of admitting that they have never been heli-skiing. It would be the equivalent of a fly fisherman recklessly conceding that he had never yanked a 30-pound wild salmon out of the River Spey. Not that there are any left now, but that's not the point either.

If you want to hold your own in skiing circles you must embrace the whole heli-ski experience with gusto and bravado. So, first: where have you been? You can confidently drop the Cariboos, the Bugaboos, the Caucasus and the Himalayas into the conversation in the certain knowledge that your audience will nod sagely, stroking their chins ruminatively with approval. You'll be on relatively safe ground as long as you remember where they are (Canada for the first two, Georgia – the ex-Soviet one – and India or, er, possibly Nepal).

Lie blithely about the identity of your heli-operator, in case someone has actually travelled with the one you claim to know about. In other words, make it up. Something vaguely credible like 'Wild Wings' will serve the purpose admirably – but check online first that it doesn't actually exist. In fact, say that you found it on an alternative ski website called outer-limits.com, and that you were particularly intrigued to learn that it was staffed by Russian ex-special forces combatants. 'You must meet my old friend, Yuri,' you might say with a fond smile. 'Ask him about that time we skied off a cornice in Kazakhstan and then realised that he'd forgotten his parachute. Fortunately I managed to bring him down on mine. He should be out of plaster by now. How we laughed!'

If you really want to push your luck, claim to have flown the 'bird' yourself. 'What a blast,' you might tell an initially sceptical audience. 'A truly wonderful bucketing ride in a 30-year-old Kamov Ka-50 Black Shark I picked up for $400 in Tashkent. It still had bullet holes from Chechnya in the fuselage. Now, that's what I call flying!'

Then there are certain key expressions that must feature firmly in your heli-skiing vocabulary. First, remind your audience of the central axiom of extreme skiing: 'There are no friends on powder days.'

'I make no apologies,' you might continue with disarming candour. 'But when you get that first glimpse of a blanket of fresh powder on a steep couloir at 20,000 feet, you discover the meaning of oneness. You just go for it, devouring the stuff like a starving man.' In fact, in the unlikely event that you ever do find yourself in such circumstances, that's exactly what would happen – with your lower jaw shovelling the snow into your mouth as you slide uncontrollably, face down, head first, for more vertical feet than you can possibly imagine – see below.

Next, remember the words 'safety first', and speak with authority about the inherent dangers of heli-skiing. 'I don't want to alarm you,' you might confide gravely, 'but I once saw a German banker neatly decapitated by the main rotor. I can still see Ludwig's frozen smile as I picked up his head. Never, ever jump up to catch your hat when you're standing under the blades. It was his first – and, sadly, his last – mistake.'

And then of course there is what must always be known as 'vertical' (sometimes also known as 'vert'). The average amount of vertical feet in a heli-skiing day is said to be about 25,000, or 'just under an Everest'. The record for the most vert in a day, if you can believe it, is allegedly 325,000 feet. You should never claim to have done more than 200,000. Inevitably some poor, deluded fools claim to have done 400,000, but you will shake your head sadly as you recount this, saying: 'Altitude sickness can play havoc with the mind.'

Next you will also need to talk about your equipment (the skiing sort). You will always carry a Pieps DSP (avalanche transceiver) specially adapted with the addition of an FM transmitter for detection by the helicopter pilot at long range, and an avalanche airbag, also specially adapted to accommodate shovel, avalanche probe and Ludwig's head. You will also carry an Avocet watch for checking your vertical, equally specially adapted (naturally) to read beyond the maximum scale.

Be careful about boasting about how high the 'drop' point is, especially if you claim that it's above 20,000 feet. But keep your nerve if some know-it-all points out that helicopters tend to crash above this height because the air is so thin. Just smile knowingly and say confidently: 'Above 20,000 I only ever fly in specially adapted, high-altitude stealth 'copters.'

With all this experience of helicopters behind you, you might also add that your favourite film is *Apocalypse Now*; every heli-skier talks about the ultimate 'chopper' film. If you feel up to it you can even do a passable impression of the soundtrack by beating your chest very quickly for a surprisingly authentic throb of rotor blades, repeating darkly: 'The horror. The horror.' For light relief, you could add the actor Robert Duvall's memorable line: 'I love the smell of napalm in the morning.' Don't say this in front of your pilot, because he will have heard it a thousand times before and this might just be the day that he cracks and flies you all into the side of the mountain.

And that's all you really need to know about heli-skiing. Except that one day, even bluffers really should give it a whirl.

Of course you want a suntan.
It makes you look good and looking
good is the whole point of the
exercise. But you must never admit
that it is a consideration.

CHOOSING A RESORT

ESSENTIAL CRITERIA
Claim to be guided by three considerations:

ALTITUDE
The higher the better; there is more snow at altitude. You will know that the resort height is not as crucial as the height of the 'top station', which should be well above the tree line. This needn't be so in the USA where the tree line is twice as high as in the Alps. If you want to be disparaging about a choice of resort it's usually safe to say: 'Too low', except in Colorado, parts of the Tarentaise in France, much of Switzerland and around Mont Blanc.

TOUGH SKIING TERRAIN
Vital for bluffers – even if they have no intention of going anywhere near it.

SNOW RECORD AND CONDITIONS
You will be expected to know all about this. Current conditions can be found in some newspapers, TV weather

reports, by visiting ski websites or spending a fortune ringing a snowline. Historic conditions need only be alluded to, but it is useful to be able to say: 'Such-and-such had 40 feet of snow last season.'

Depth of snow is all-important. You must know that 12 centimetres (just under five inches) is the absolute minimum to ski on, but considerably more than that is preferable as an ideal 'base'. Finally, 'direction of slopes' is a vital constituent. Snow 'holds up' better on north-facing slopes than south-facing ones because they spend less time in the sun. A surfeit of north-facing slopes in a resort is therefore a good thing. But not if you want a suntan.

NON-ESSENTIAL CRITERIA

A SUNTAN

Of course you want a suntan. It makes you look good and, as previously observed, looking good is the whole point of the exercise. But you must never admit that it is a consideration. If you do manage to get one, ensure that you don't get 'panda eyes' – white patches caused by over-reliance on UV-blocking sunglasses and goggles. Admittedly, many instructors have them – but it's not a good look.

ALPINE CHARM

This, of course, is a prerequisite for the majority of skiers – who must never admit to it either. 'What on earth has the architecture got to do with the skiing?' you will scoff – perhaps adding dismissively: 'After all, we are here to ski, are we not?' Nobody will dare dispute this and anybody who admits to being influenced by a desire for chocolate-box prettiness can be justifiably vilified, however much you may agree with them. There is ample scope here to be deliberately provocative and claim that the ugliest resorts (nearly always French) are the best. This shows that you take your skiing seriously.

VALUE FOR MONEY

Skiing is an expensive business. The dedicated skier would never admit to being bothered by budgetary considerations.

COUNTRIES

The main centres of world skiing – not necessarily in order of importance – are as follows:

SWITZERLAND

This is where it all started. It has some of the most delightful, most fashionable and most ruinously expensive resorts in the world. Declare that nothing beats it. Resorts you must claim to have skied include Zermatt (the new celebrity magnet), Klosters (very popular with royals), Mürren (where Arnold Lunn invented slalom skiing) and St Moritz (simply because everyone will have heard of it). Dismiss Gstaad as 'past it' and too low.

FRANCE

Magnificent skiing, the largest linked ski areas in the world and resorts mostly purpose-built and post-war (designed by exponents of the Brutalist school of French architecture). Talk passionately about the limitless skiing terrain and remember to drop the name 'Michaud'. He was the engineer appointed by de Gaulle to wreak wholesale concrete blight on the French Alps. Say firmly that Val d'Isère (known simply as 'Val') is the ultimate skiers' resort, that Chamonix is where the cognoscenti go, and that Courchevel 1850 is probably the most hedonistic destination in skiing – especially for obscenely rich Russians.

AUSTRIA

Hot on Alpine charm, good for skiing at all levels, value for money (comparatively), frenetic *lederhosen*-lowering après-ski and fruit-flavoured schnapps. Say that for 'all-round' attraction it is hard to beat but caution that many of the resorts tend to be on the low side. However, this is not true of St Anton, a serious experts' resort because of the huge amount of off-piste skiing and therefore not recommended for nervous bluffers who might be better off heading for historic and very pretty Kitzbühel. Or perhaps Ischgl, which has more lap-dancing clubs than any other ski resort in Europe.

ITALY

Traditionally chaotic and undisciplined, many Italian resorts have usurped the concept of après-ski and shown the French how it should be done. Italians also know a thing or two about looking good. Insist that for constant entertainment and beautiful people, nothing beats it. Of the skiing, you will scratch your head and say: 'Can be wonderfully scenic.' This is especially true of the Dolomites (Cortina d'Ampezzo is the fashionable mecca to head for) and Cervinia on the Italian-Swiss border (maximum bluffing points for anyone who points out that it was designed by Mussolini as a state-of-the-art winter playground in the 1930s). For those partial to bars, and even more bars, party towns don't come much more riotous than Sauze d'Oulx. Even its name sounds like an advanced state of stimulant-induced cognitive dysfunction.

♛

Insist that for constant entertainment and beautiful people, nothing beats Italy.

USA

In any conversation about skiing in the USA or Canada, sigh wistfully at any mention of the Rockies. Unbelievably high, some resorts in Colorado are close to 10,000 feet – skiing well over 12,000 feet. There are more than 1,500 resorts/ski areas spread from east to west coast in the USA and Canada, so you might confidently claim to have skied the most obscure of them, especially if they sound genuinely terrifying. Be sure of your ground here, though. If you insist on impressing your audience with your exploits on

'Suicide Six', and someone googles it for verification, they'll discover that it's a family-friendly resort in Vermont with some equally friendly nursery slopes. Best to stick to the big ones such as Aspen and Telluride in Colorado, authentic old mining towns with some impressive mountains. Some valuable bluffing observations here: Aspen has its own rugby (union) club, founded by an Englishman in 1967. The pitch is in the centre of the town, making it arguably the most valuable acre of sporting real estate in the world. Telluride, up there with Aspen in the glamour stakes, was where Butch Cassidy carried out his first ever bank job. And in the late 1800s it also had more brothels per capita than any other community in America.

The other must-ski resort in the USA – one you will naturally claim to have visited – is Jackson Hole, in the cowboy town of Jackson, Wyoming. This experts' ski area is home to the infamous Corbet's Couloir, which not even the most reckless of bluffers should be seen anywhere near.

CANADA

The location of unquestionably the best heli-skiing in the world (*see* Glossary), Canada is therefore essential bluffing territory. You will have skied with wolves, bears, coyotes, bankers…and other scavenging predators. Just mention the word 'Bugaboos' and that should be enough.

You must have skied in Whistler, so-called in 1900 by early settlers because of the shrill whistle sound made by the hoary marmots in the surrounding mountains. It was a close-run thing when it came to choosing a suitable name;

there was strong support for 'Hoary Mountain', which might have held it back from being consistently voted among the world's top five resorts. And you should not overlook Banff Lake Louise, not only one of the most scenic ski areas in the world, but also the location of Delirium Dive – another of North America's most infamous 'steeps'.

OTHER COUNTRIES

You will also be required to have a comprehensive knowledge of other skiing destinations around the world, including some of the more exotic ones:

AUSTRALIA AND NEW ZEALAND

Australians obstinately insist that September is 'springtime'. This is therefore their peak skiing season. Generally speaking their skiing areas suffer from lack of altitude, which explains why so few Australian skiers live in Australia. However, comment favourably on the unusual experience of skiing amid exotic birdlife and enormous spiders. The Snowy Mountains are the main focus of skiing, and you should refer to the exotically named ski areas of Thredbo, Perisher, Blue Cow and Smiggin Holes.

The main thing to know about New Zealand is that the country has barely tapped its enormous skiing potential, and if only the Kiwis would get on with developing it instead of bungee jumping and sheep farming (not necessarily at the same time), then the skiing in the Southern Alps would compare with the best of the original Alps. Mention Mount Hutt and The Remarkables.

SOUTH AMERICA

Chile and Argentina traditionally look for any excuse for a fight and nothing exercises them more than an argument about who has the best skiing. Stay well clear of these arguments but wax lyrical about the Andes if asked to venture an opinion. Mention Cerro Catedral and Las Leñas in Argentina, and Portillo in Chile.

ASIA

The continent affords marvellous opportunities for bluffing about skiing in Lebanon, Georgia, Turkey, Iraq, India and Japan. It is a little-known fact, for example, that Lebanon's four ski resorts remained open throughout the civil war in the 1970s and 1980s. Naturally you will have skied in all of these (especially Cedars of Lebanon) and will talk about the thrill of skiing 'under mortar fire'. In Georgia you will have gone heli-skiing in the Caucasus; in Turkey you will talk of Uludağ (formerly Olympus) and the proximity of the Sea of Marmara; and in India you will have been mesmerised by the Himalayas and their incalculable skiing potential. You might also talk with impressive authority about the Kashmir problem, and how you are working quietly to resolve it.

SCANDINAVIA

Interesting skiing if you're not planning too much in the way of downhill. You will talk in hushed tones about skiing under the Midnight Sun, or the Northern Lights, or the influence of alcohol. Or all three. You will also claim to have been chased by wolves across the snowy wildernesses of Norway, Sweden, Finland and Lapland.

SPAIN
Here, you will of course have skied with King Juan Carlos in Baqueira-Beret. Or avoided pigs-on-planks in the Sierra Nevada, near Torremolinos.

SCOTLAND
Famed for having the least reliable snow record, the worst weather, the shortest runs and the least inviting mountain restaurants, Scotland is a profoundly tough place to go skiing – and therefore must be stoutly supported by bluffers who insist that they enjoy a challenge. Suggest that Nevis Range (which used to be called Aonach Mor until the local tourist office realised that no one could pronounce it) would be superb. If it had more snow.

EASTERN EUROPE
You will have skied in the High Tatras between Poland and Slovakia, and in Bulgaria and Romania (but only briefly). You will sound optimistic about the future of Slovenia, Montenegro and Serbia, but venture knowledgeably that all the investment is heading further east towards Russia – especially Sochi, the host town of the 2014 Winter Olympics and a personal favourite of Vladimir Putin.

Downhill skiing is the most fun to watch, especially if you're one of those people who slows down to get a closer view of a car crash.

COMPETITIVE SKIING

All skiers are competitive, but some are more competitive than others. It's a good idea to know something about competition skiing, particularly ski racing, so that you can venture the odd informed opinion about the classic races. Only three disciplines really count: downhill, slalom and giant slalom.

DOWNHILL

This is the most fun to watch, especially if you're one of those people who slows down to get a closer view of a car crash. The courses are between two and three miles long for men, about two miles for women. Both will expect to finish in under two minutes at average speeds of 70mph for men and 60mph for women. Vertical drops range from 500 to 1,000 metres. When contestants fly past (sometimes airborne for more than 50 metres at over 90mph), no one hears them scream because spectators are required to shout: 'Hup! Hup! Hup!' (a curious exhortation considering they are trying to come down).

Downhill racing is the most suicidal of the disciplines

but success confers undreamt-of prestige. Nations weep with pride, clasp downhill champions to their bosoms (figuratively speaking) and think of them as favoured children. The British don't do this because it is not in the national character. The fact that the British have never had a downhill champion has absolutely nothing to do with it.

SLALOM

This is a race on a very steep, short, icy section of piste, which requires men to pass between 55 and 75 gates, and women between 45 and 65. The idea is to see how many red and blue poles they can uproot, and who can do it the quickest. The race is run over two legs.

GIANT SLALOM

Similar to slalom but run over a longer course at higher speeds. Two legs of about 90 seconds each. Even more contestants impale themselves than before.

COMPETITIONS

Only three skiing competitions really count: the Winter Olympics (every four years), the World Championships (every two years) and the World Cup (every year) – the Grand Prix of ski racing. The Olympic downhill is the big one, where one-hundredth of a second can mean the difference between obscurity and immortality.

There are two great World Cup classics:

The Hahnenkamm Held in Kitzbühel, Austria, this is so frightening that hardened racers have to be dragged kicking and screaming to the starting line where they're pushed over a vertical drop, freefall for about 10 seconds and spend the rest of the course fighting to regain control of their skis (and their bowels).

The Lauberhorn Held in Wengen, Switzerland, this is, by comparison, a pleasant Sunday afternoon stroll – at 80mph. The oldest of the courses, it has some infamous sections, amusingly named after scenes of national disasters. (Never joke about Canadian Corner or Austrian Hole to ski racers from either country.) Celebrated Swiss skier Peter Müller had a spectacular crash on the jump into the finish. He survived, but about 10 hay bales were vapourised.

The other major World Cup races are held in Val d'Isère (France), Garmisch (Germany), Val Gardena (Italy) and Aspen (USA). They can safely be called 'tough, but not too tough'.

First-timers are to be deeply envied. No skier will ever again have as much fun falling over and laughing uncontrollably at everything.

SKI TYPES

B luffers must be able to recognise certain categories of skier, if only to confirm which are fellow bluffers and which are not.

THE MOUNTAIN LEGEND

There is no terrain he hasn't skied, no challenge he hasn't conquered, no crevasse he hasn't been in, no avalanche he hasn't 'raced', no cliff he hasn't jumped. He skis in powder so deep he needs a periscope to see where he's going. He makes these claims in the knowledge that no one can refute them because no one has ever seen him ski. That is because he 'must ski alone': the danger gives him an adrenaline 'buzz'. He wears an avalanche transceiver on the outside of his suit (£700 worth of zips and buckles), guaranteed pristine at all times.

THE HOT ROD

He rarely skis because he can't afford to spend that long away from a mirror. He notches up female victims on his skis like a fighter pilot on his fuselage. If asked why he doesn't ski he will say that he's 'bored' with it. In fact he could never get the hang of it. If a flea were to dive into his pool of skiing knowledge, it would break its neck.

THE SNOW KITTEN

Kittens hang around hot rods looking thin and pained. This is because hot rods don't pay them any attention and kittens don't know what else to do. Like hot rods, they are keen on suntans and video bars and not too keen on snow. They are also keen on fur, Ferraris, fat wallets and people called Fabio. They aren't too clever, though; they usually fail to notice that Fabio hasn't got any money.

THE FREELOADER

Freeloaders are generally ski journalists; self-appointed epicureans who rarely ski, not because they can't but because they prefer to remain in bars and ventilate pompously on their coverage of 'hot' new resorts called Trucktown Ski Station or Sans-Neige, places so unappealing that even ski writers wouldn't accept an invitation to visit them; even with the promise of an upgrade to first class – usually a reliable inducement.

THE PIG-ON-PLANKS

PoPs are notoriously violent; with little provocation they would stick a ski in your mouth – sideways. They tend to have thick necks and no brains; they can often be seen trying to figure out how to work a zip. On skis they exhibit all the characteristics of a hit-and-run driver.

Their technique hasn't progressed beyond a 60mph snowplough, and they couldn't stop even if they wanted to. Unfortunately they are nearly always British.

INSTRUCTORS AND GUIDES

Male ski instructors are dangerous. They are over-sexed, amoral, utterly ruthless, vain, impatient and irresistible to women. The lucky bastards. Male ski guides are even more deadly. Unlike instructors they are required to be polite and therefore create a false sense of security. They humiliate clients by rescuing them after luring them into tricky situations. This impresses female clients who find them even more irresistible than instructors.

Female instructors wear expressions of extreme boredom brought about by years of exposure to small children on skis, and pigs-on-planks who should know better than to try to molest them. They are among the most dangerous women in the world to molest. If you try it they can effortlessly kill you and make it look like an accident.

THE PISTEUR/SKI PATROLMAN

Charged with the task of keeping order on the slopes and clearing them of bodies after a day's skiing, pisteurs are either frustrated policemen or would-be instructors who didn't make the grade. They are generally angry about everything. Occasionally they have to do something mundane like rope off a section of piste. This makes them angrier than ever.

In the USA ski 'patrolmen' wear mirrored sunglasses and feel that they should be allowed to shoot people. They make do with hiding in trees to catch people speeding, then clamp a flashing blue light to their hats and set off in hot pursuit.

THE ARTIFICIER

Highest grade of pisteur – i.e., those qualified to use explosives to 'aid' avalanches and blow up persistent offenders. It is not a good idea to smoke too near them, or do anything that might incur their displeasure.

THE SKI BUM

Professional spongers who hang around resorts sleeping uninvited on chalet girls' floors, depleting the week's food and drink stock, latching on to groups of guests in the hope of a free drink and, on the rare occasions that they crawl out of bed in time, spending their time on the mountain (courtesy of a borrowed lift pass) clutching their heads and whining pitifully.

THE FIRST-TIMER

First-timers are to be deeply envied. No skier will ever again have as much fun falling over and laughing uncontrollably at everything. First-timers are made conspicuous by their verbal diarrhoea, permanent grins and muddy backsides.

There's no point in pretending that you know everything about skiing – nobody does – but if you've got this far and you've absorbed at least a modicum of the information and advice contained within these pages, then you will almost certainly know more than 99% of the rest of the human race about what skiing is, why people enjoy it, and how you can pretend to be better at it than you are. What you now do with this information is up to you, but here's a suggestion: be confident about your newfound knowledge, see how far it takes you, but above all, have fun using it.

And don't ever try to look good skiing on ice.

GLOSSARY

Abfahrt German for 'descent', much in evidence on signs in Switzerland, Austria and Germany. A source of endless amusement to English-speaking children of all ages.

Air Something that all bluffers must claim they like to 'catch' when soaring through it (usually unintentionally).

Apartment Small cupboard in the French Alps. Useful for storing a pair of ski boots and not much else.

Boilerplate Ice that is formed from freezing water rather than compressed snow. Skiing on a china plate would be easier.

Bottleneck Mayhem encountered in: a) a section of piste that is too narrow for ski traffic; b) a permanent lift queue.

Bowl Any treeless expanse of skiing terrain that looks like a bowl. 'Back' bowls are more in vogue than any other sort because they suggest that they are some distance from help. This is often the case.

Caught-an-edge Fell over.

Caulfeild, Vivian Seminal early British ski writer, author of *How to Ski* (1910). Famous for spelling 'field' wrong.

Chalet-hotel Hybrid form of accommodation that has all the disadvantages of hotels and none of the advantages of chalets (like unlimited free wine).

Counter-rotation Alarming physical phenomenon in which the upper body turns the opposite way from the lower body during a skiing manoeuvre.

Crud Thick, sticky, glutinous chunks of old powder snow like grey goulash. Difficult to imagine how it got its name.

DIN Loud noise. Acronym for German standards organisation with disproportionate influence on ski design.

Drag lift Any ski lift that drags skiers up a mountain in maximum discomfort.

Flapping What a soft ski does at speed on hard snow. Also what the most irritating member of your party does all the time.

Foam injection Excruciatingly painful means of providing ski boots with a 'perfect' moulded fit. Don't believe it.

Gunbarrel 'U'-shaped piste with high curving sides and a carpet of moguls. You'd be better off looking into the other sort.

Heli-skiing Expensive form of ski lift. Heli-skiers hum *The Ride of the Valkyries* once airborne, much to the irritation of the pilot.

Hooking Increasingly popular justification for falling over due to over-sharpened edges that 'hook' the snow.

Hot-dog Freestyle skiing discipline that has something to do with moguls and nothing to do with sausages.

Inner skiing Quaint theory about discovering skiing technique from within. Worth trying if all else fails.

Le fart French for ski wax; English speakers find it even more entertaining than the German for descent.

Linked Connecting pistes by ski lifts, or connecting turns by not falling over.

Magic carpet Rolling synthetic surface under a chairlift on which skiers must remain motionless while waiting for the chair to smack into the back of their legs. Unnerving.

Miller, Warren US director of extreme ski movies able to persuade fit young men to hurl themselves off precipices and land in wheelchairs.

Moonboot Form of footwear that makes the wearer look like a Hobbit.

Motorway Name given to wide, easy cruising pistes much loved by bluffers.

Piste map Remarkable example of origami.

Pre-release Great excuse for falling over due to boots prematurely detaching from bindings.

Pschitt Brand of soft fizzy drink with a silent 'P'. Immensely popular with English-speaking children who demand it, loudly, all the time.

Rep Someone to blame when there isn't any snow. Or to blame anyway.

Sidecut Something to do with the turning radius of a ski. Either 'deep' (curvy shape) for short turns or 'shallow' (straighter shape) for longer turns. Irrelevant if you can't manage either.

Ski evolutif French theory that skiers are descended from apes. They graduated from short skis to long skis in evolutionary stages.

Snow chains Means of securing recalcitrant children in rear seats on ski-drive holidays. Also to wrap around tyres in icy conditions (chains, not children).

Transfer Innocuous name given to an interminable coach journey between airport and resort.

Wipeout Popular means of describing inability to remain upright and still attached to one's skis.

Yellow snow Curious meteorological phenomenon found near lift attendants' huts, or mountain restaurants that restrict the use of toilets to customers only. Not to be investigated too closely.

Zdarsky, Mathias The 'father' of Alpine skiing. He wrote *Lilienfelder Skilauf-Technik* (1896). Should be beside every ski bluffer's bedside.

BLUFFING NOTES

Bluffing Notes

Bluffing Notes

Bluffing Notes

Bluffing Notes

Bluffing Notes

Bluffing Notes

THE Bluffer's® GUIDE TO

THE HEADLINES

SIGN UP FOR YOUR
FREE WEEKLY DIGEST AT
BLUFFERS.COM!

Every Friday, receive our essential
news recap: a bluffer's must-have guide
to who did what and what happened
when during the week that was.

BLUFFERS.COM

FOLLOW US ON TWITTER:
@BLUFFERSGUIDE

LIKE US ON FACEBOOK:
FACEBOOK.COM/BLUFFERSGUIDES

COMING SOON

Become an instant expert with these new
and forthcoming Bluffer's Guides®.

NEW EDITIONS

BEER
CARS
CRICKET
CYCLING
DOGS
FOOTBALL
GOLF
HIKING
INSIDER HOLLYWOOD
JAZZ
MANAGEMENT
OPERA

POETRY
QUANTUM UNIVERSE
RACES
ROCK MUSIC
RUGBY
SAILING
SEX
SKIING
SURFING
TENNIS
WINE
YOUR OWN BUSINESS

BLUFFERS.COM
@BLUFFERSGUIDE